D1546125

I can't pinpoint exactly when my aphoristic obsession began; perhaps it was elementary school. I remember borrowing a couple of jokes from *The Muppet Show* and trying them out on my friends one wintry morning as we waited for the first bell to call us to class. I got a big laugh, even though I'm fairly sure my classmates knew I wasn't working with original material.

In college, I developed the habit of scribbling my favorite bits of pithy wisdom onto index cards that I taped to the wall above my desk. The cards became popular enough that I would often return from class to find my roommates and their friends standing in my dorm room giggling at one phrase or another. Over the years since then, throughout my writing career, I've kept a carefully tended folder of my favorite quotes related to all manner of subjects: work, food, cinema, men and women, politics and religion, romance, art, and money—but especially about sex. From politicians to porn stars

> I quote others only to better express myself.

MICHEL DE MONTAIGNE

and Nobel laureates to musicians, from the notable to the unknown, across the centuries and disparate cultures, sex and sexuality with all of its permutations, quirks and mystery is what binds us together. We are all one beneath the sheets. In this collection you will find a wide variety of aphorisms designed to amuse and stimulate—in every sense of the word. I ask only that you pass along the quotes that you find most illuminating. After all, isn't that what an oral history— wink, nudge—is all about? Enjoy! *Viel Spaß!*

JC Adams
Los Angeles, California, USA
March 2013

SEX AND SOCIETY

It doesn't matter what
you do in the bedroom
as long as you don't do it in the street
and frighten the horses.

MRS. CAMPBELL, HUMORIST

Sex is not a frill; it's not a luxury.
It's part of your life whether you're
flush or famished, living under
dictators or Democrats. It has its own
unique relationship to history and
it will not shut up.

SUSIE BRIGHT, AUTHOR AND ACTIVIST

Sex is a big question mark.
It is something people will
talk about forever.

CATHERINE
DENEUVE
actress

Don't bother discussing sex with small children.
They rarely have anything to add.

FRAN LEBOWITZ, HUMORIST

All fashionable vices pass for virtues.

MOLIÈRE
playwright

I'm interested in the modern suggestion that
you can have a combination of love and sex
in a marriage—which no previous society
has ever believed.

ALAIN DE BOTTON, AUTHOR AND PHILOSOPHER

Romantic love:
nature's way of duping us
into reproducing our species.

ARTHUR SCHOPENHAUER, PHILOSOPHER

Social confusion has now reached a point
at which the pursuit of immorality turns out to be more
exhausting than compliance with the old moral codes.

DENIS
DIDEROT
critic, philosopher

I've become somewhat notorious…

for my positions on HIV.

To put it as briefly as possible: I can't quite believe

it's a curse. I'm not trying to out-Louise Ms.

Hay, but in my life, AIDS has been an undeniable blessing.

It woke me up to what was important; it let me know

that now was the time to do it. And—this is the part

that upsets people—it also gives me the freedom

to behave "irresponsibly." I look at the HIV-negative

people around me, and I pity them. They live their lives

in constant fear of infection: mustn't do this,

mustn't do that, mustn't take risks. They can't see

past "avoidance of infection," which has come to be

their ultimate goal… My life is so much more carefree

than theirs, so much more "considered," that I shake

my head and count myself lucky to have been infected.

Risk taking is the essence of life, and people

who spend their entire lives trying to eliminate risk from

their lives are… well, they're not my kind of people.

SCOTT
O'HARA
porn actor, activist

There is a charm about the forbidden
that makes it unspeakably desirable.

MARK TWAIN, AUTHOR AND WIT

Money, it turned out, was exactly like sex—
you thought of nothing else if you didn't have it
and thought of other things if you did.

JAMES
BALDWIN
author, critic

We know that more than seventy to eighty percent
of women masturbate, and ninety percent
of men masturbate, and the rest lie.

JOYCELYN ELDERS, FORMER U.S. SURGEON GENERAL

I never considered myself trashy or slutty;
I consider myself nasty and sexy. Big difference.

DIESEL
WASHINGTON
porn actor

I do earnestly wish to see the distinction of sex confounded
in society, unless where love animates the behavior.

MARY WOLLSTONECRAFT, AUTHOR, ACTIVIST, AND PHILOSOPHER

Sex is an emotion in motion.

MAE WEST

actress, satirist

When people are fed and clothed, then they think about sex.

CONFUCIUS, PHILOSOPHER

Sexuality poorly repressed unsettles some families; well repressed, it unsettles the whole world.

KARL
KRAUS

author satirist

Being a personal trainer, you have to scarf down food between clients. I ate my meal in three minutes and I want more. Now I understand every Taylor Swift song.

MATTHEW RUSH, PORN ACTOR

I'd never seen men hold each other. I thought the only thing they were allowed to do was shake hands or fight.

RITA MAE BROWN, AUTHOR

As soon as it becomes a right, you can't do it anymore. Self-consciousness, you see.

STEPHEN
FRY

author actor

Rock is really about dick and testosterone.

I go see a band, I want to fuck the guy. That's the way it is.

It's always been that way.

COURTNEY LOVE
musician, singer

It is certainly very hard to write about sex in English without
making it unattractive.

EDMUND WILSON, AUTHOR AND SOCIAL CRITIC

Really, to sin you have to be serious about it.

HENRIK IBSEN, PLAYWRIGHT

Science is a lot like sex. Sometimes something useful comes
of it, but that's not the reason we're doing it.

RICHARD FEYNMAN, PHYSICIST

Sophisticated persons masturbate without compunction.
They do it for reasons of health, privacy, thrift, and because of
the remarkable perfection of invisible partners.

P.J. O'ROURKE, AUTHOR AND SATIRIST

I'd like to meet the man who invented sex and see what he's working on now.

UNKNOWN ORIGIN

To speak of morals in art is to speak of legislature in sex. Art is the sex of the imagination.

GEORGE JEAN NATHAN, DRAMA CRITIC AND PUBLISHER

What holds the world together, as I have learned from bitter experience, is sexual intercourse.

There is object proof that homosexuality is more interesting than heterosexuality. It's that one knows a considerable number of heterosexuals who would wish to become homosexuals, whereas one knows very few homosexuals who would really like to become heterosexuals.

MICHEL FOUCAULT, PHILOSOPHER

Literature—creative literature—unconcerned
with sex, is inconceivable.

GERTRUDE STEIN, AUTHOR AND THINKER

Drinking when we are not thirsty and making love at any time,
madame; that is all there is to distinguish us from the other
animals. (*The Marriage of Figaro*)

PIERRE BEAUMARCHAIS, AUTHOR

Eroticism is firstly a search for pleasure, a perception of the
divine state, which is infinite delight.

ALAIN DANIÉLOU, HISTORIAN

The vice is not in entering, but in
not coming out again. (Response to students
who saw him enter the house of a prostitute.)

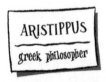

Give me the luxuries of life and I will willingly do
without the necessities.

FRANK LLOYD WRIGHT, ARCHITECT AND DESIGNER

Sex is. There is nothing more to be done about it.
Sex builds no roads, writes no novels and sex certainly gives no
meaning to anything in life but itself.

GORE
VIDAL
author

If sex isn't a joke, what is?

NELLA LARSEN, AUTHOR

Like sex in Victorian England, the reality
of Big Business today is our big dirty secret.

RALPH NADER, CONSUMER ADVOCATE

As a culture I see us as presently deprived of subtleties.
The music is loud, the anger is elevated,
sex seems lacking in sweetness and privacy.

SHELLEY BERMAN, HUMORIST

We live in a world that is saturated in sexual suggestion,
but not sex itself.

CONNER HABIB, PORN ACTOR AND AUTHOR

It seems to me that the real clue to your sex-orientation lies

in your romantic feelings rather than in your sexual feelings.
If you are really gay, you are able to fall in love with a man,
not just enjoy having sex with him.

CHRISTOPHER ISHERWOOD, AUTHOR

You know, music is sex. It's a sensual, driving mode that affects
people if it's played a certain way.

Just because you're offended doesn't mean you're right.

RICKY GERVAIS, COMEDIAN

I believe in using words, not fists. I believe in my outrage
knowing people are living in boxes on the street.
I believe in honesty. I believe in a good time.
I believe in good food. I believe in sex.

BERTRAND RUSSELL, CRITIC AND PHILOSOPHER

My sexuality has never been a problem to me,
but I think it has been for other people.

DUSTY SPRINGFIELD, SINGER

Smoking is very bad for you and should only be done because it looks so good. People who don't smoke have a terrible time finding something polite to do with their lips.

P.J. O'Rourke, author and satirist

I wanted it to be sexual because rock and roll is about sexuality. And I felt that by being blunt, it would disarm people. People were trying to assimilate at that time. It was the time of AIDS, and people felt, we can't misbehave because we want straight people to support us over this important issue. And I said, I see your point but I disagree. I think we should be as bold and as out and upfront as possible, and that people will respect us for that. To not be cowed, to not be cautious, about what people might think. Because if you're always worried about what people might think it's going to inhibit you, and I wanted to have honest expression. And I thought, I can do this. It's my sense of humor, and using that, I can get this message across.

Jon Ginoli, Pansy Division singer

When anything is made, people will find a way to see their reflection in it. As soon as their reflection appears, they'll want to fuck it.

Paul Constant, journalist and blogger

The space between what reality TV offers and just watching people have sex has collapsed over time, which was perhaps inevitable for two genres that blur fantasy and documentary, asking subjects to expose what are usually secret parts of themselves in artificial contexts. Our attraction to reality TV stars' private lives has led to the inevitable, as reality TV begins to embrace porn and porn embraces reality TV.

ANDY DEHNART, TELEVISION CRITIC

It is the function of vice to keep virtue within reasonable bounds.

SAMUEL BUTLER, NOVELIST

We live in a world where traditional labels don't apply anymore, partly as a result of gay emancipation. Being gay is not taboo anymore, and I'd say at least thirty percent of city boys in the Central European region happily experiment with their sexuality. Many enjoy it, but they wouldn't think of themselves as being gay.

GEORGE DUROY, ADULT FILMMAKER

It's just gossip, you know. Gossip is the new pornography.

WOODY ALLEN, FILMMAKER

I decided law was the exact opposite of sex;
even when it was good, it was lousy.

MORTIMER ZUCKERMAN, PUBLISHER AND REAL ESTATE MOGUL

A promiscuous person is usually someone who
is getting more sex than you are.

VICTOR LOWNES, FORMER PLAYBOY ENTERPRISES EXECUTIVE

Genitals are a great distraction to scholarship.

MALCOLM BRADBURY, AUTHOR AND EDUCATOR

We're supposed to procreate and society, God knows, is
ferocious on the subject. Heterosexuality is considered such a
great and natural good that you have to execute people and put
them in prison if they don't practice this glorious act.

GORE VIDAL, AUTHOR

Sex is a doorway to something so powerful and mystical, but
movies usually depict it in a completely flat way.

DAVID
LYNCH
filmmaker

Pleasure's a sin, and sometimes sin's a pleasure.

LORD BYRON, POET AND LOVER

I always thought of losing my virginity as a career move.

MADONNA
singer, filmmaker

Sex appeal is the keynote of our civilization.

HENRI-LOUIS BERGSON, PHILOSOPHER

Masturbation is the thinking man's television.

CHRISTOPHER HAMPTON, DRAMATIST AND FILMMAKER

This is the way I look at sex scenes: I have basically been doing them for a living for years. Trying to seduce an audience is the basis of rock 'n' roll, and if I may say so, I'm pretty good at it.

JON BON JOVI, SINGER, MUSICIAN, AND ACTOR

Sex is as important as eating or drinking and
we ought to allow the one appetite to be satisfied with as little
restraint or false modesty as the other.

MARQUIS DE SADE, AUTHOR, PHILOSOPHER, AND LOVER

Sex is not only the basis of life, it is the reason for life.

NORMAN LINDSAY, ARTIST

A laugh at sex is a laugh at destiny.

THORNTON WILDER, PLAYWRIGHT AND NOVELIST

If some really acute observer made as much of egotism as Freud has made of sex, people would forget a good deal about sex and find the explanation for everything in egotism.

These pleasures so lightly called physical...

COLETTE, AUTHOR

Self-denial is not a virtue:

it is the only effect of prudence on rascality.

GEORGE BERNARD SHAW, PLAYWRIGHT AND JOURNALIST

Amazing that the human race has taken enough time out from thinking about food or sex to create the arts and sciences.

MASON COOLEY, AUTHOR AND APHORIST

Deviant (definition):

A person who wanders from the One True Path

and is caught urinating somewhere in the midst

of the unthinkable. A person taking any exit ramp

off the freeway of self-righteousness.

RICHARD SUMMERBELL, AUTHOR

Bed is the poor man's opera.

UNKNOWN ORIGIN

I am still of opinion that only two topics can be of the least

interest to a serious and studious mood: sex and the dead.

WILLIAM BUTLER YEATS, POET

It's hard to be funny when you have to be clean.

MAE WEST, ACTRESS, FILMMAKER, AND SATIRIST

Is a gay play a play that has sex with other plays?

HARVEY FIERSTEIN
dramatist, actor

CHARLES
BUKOWSKI
poet

Sex is interesting, but it's not totally important. I mean it's not even as important, physically, as excretion. A man can go seventy years without a piece of ass, but he can die in a week without a bowel movement.

Homosexuality strikes at the heart of the organization
of Western culture and societies. Because homosexuality,
by its nature, is nonreproductive, it posits a sexuality that is
justified by pleasure alone.

A dirty book is rarely dusty.

UNKNOWN ORIGIN

Bisexuality should be the norm.
It's the cure for many problems. I don't believe in gay versus
straight. The message of the gay liberation movement should
have been freedom of sexuality, not antagonism toward
sexuality other than gay sex. Most people are going to want to
be straight, this is true, because most people breed, and nature
wants us to breed. However, I believe in the liberation of all
avenues of pleasure, and I want all straight people to have their
options open without it implicating them. The impulses are
there if they aren't repressed, so people should choose to live
without those labels.

CAMILLE PAGLIA, AUTHOR, EDUCATOR, AND SOCIAL CRITIC

What most people in our culture mean by being
lovable is essentially a mixture between being popular and
having sex appeal.

ERICH FROMM, CRITIC AND PHILOSOPHER

The ability to make love frivolously is the chief characteristic
which distinguishes human beings from beasts.

HEYWOOD BROUN, AUTHOR AND ACTIVIST

Homosexuality is God's way of insuring
that the truly gifted aren't burdened with children.

SAMUEL AUSTIN ALLIBONE, AUTHOR

Wanting sexual attention isn't a felony,
no matter how much society tries to convince [you] that it is.

SUSIE BRIGHT, AUTHOR AND ACTIVIST

I was told not to say, "I will be getting triple fisted on stage at
HustlaBall NYC" if I wasn't going to do it.

ANTHONY
ROMERO

porn actor

Sexuality is the lyricism of the masses.

CHARLES BAUDELAIRE, POET AND CRITIC

Sex is a part of nature. I go along with nature.

MARILYN MONROE, ACTRESS AND BEAUTY ICON

A pinch of notoriety will do.

QUENTIN CRISP, AUTHOR AND HUMORIST

I've tried several varieties of sex.
The conventional position makes me claustrophobic.
And the others give me either a stiff neck or lockjaw.

TALLULAH BANKHEAD, ACTRESS

My son has followed fashion since he was a punk.
He and I agree that fashion is about sex.

VIVIENNE WESTWOOD, FASHION DESIGNER

Sex is energy.

BEATRICE WOOD
artist

The decline of the celebrity sex video mirrors the diminishment
in Hollywood film of overt sex, which has migrated to pay
cable, while mainstream movies revert to prolonged rhapsodies
of renunciation such as the *Twilight* series and the dependable
tent pole of Sandra Bullock acting spunky. The porn industry
itself is on the edge of dissolution, ravaged by digital piracy that
had de-monetized and democratized porn across myriad free
Web sites where any amateur in a homemade video can attract
as many glazed eyeballs as the glossiest face on a DVD cover.
The very phrase "porn star" seems so '90s now, caked with
dried mascara. We have moved on. To where?
To wherever the all-devouring Internet takes us next.

JAMES WOLCOTT, critic

I know a man who gave up smoking, drinking, sex, and rich
food. He was healthy right up to the day he killed himself.

JOHNNY CARSON, HUMORIST

Never miss a chance to have sex or appear on television.

GORE VIDAL, AUTHOR

Sex is not the enemy.

I won't feel guilty no matter what they're telling me.

SHIRLEY MANSON, SINGER

When the authorities warn you of the dangers

of having sex, there is an important lesson to be learned:

do not have sex with the authorities.

MATT GROENING

cartoonist, filmmaker

The road of excess leads to the palace of wisdom.

WILLIAM BLAKE, POET, ARTIST, AND VISIONARY

Take care of the luxuries and the necessities

take care of themselves.

DOROTHY PARKER, AUTHOR, AND SATIRIST

Don't stay in bed, unless you can make money in bed.

GEORGE BURNS

comedian

Homosexuality was invented by a straight world
dealing with its own bisexuality.

KATE MILLETT, AUTHOR

One should always be a little improbable.

OSCAR WILDE, AUTHOR AND WIT

Life in Lubbock, Texas, taught me two things:
One is that God loves you and you're going to burn in hell.
The other is that sex is the most awful, filthy thing on earth
and you should save it for someone you love.

BUTCH
HANCOCK
singer

What I wanted to get at is the value difference
between pornographic playing-cards when you're a kid,
and pornographic playing-cards when you're older. It's that
when you're a kid you use the cards as a substitute for a real
experience, and when you're older you use real experience
as a substitute for the fantasy.

EDWARD ALBEE, PLAYWRIGHT

When choosing between two evils, I always like to try the one
I've never tried before.

MAE WEST, ACTRESS, FILMMAKER, AND SATIRIST

Erotica is the only writing genre in the world that people think
it's fair to critique even if they've never laid eyes on it.

SUSIE BRIGHT, AUTHOR AND ACTIVIST

Underneath the contempt that some people
hold about prostitution is a strong pattern of
contempt for sex. Think about it. If you believe that
sex is good by itself without needing the justification of
romance, then why shouldn't it be purchased honorably from
a man who sees himself as possessing something worthwhile?
The hustler sells an hour or so of his time, the pleasure of
his body, and an impression of intimacy. So long as he and
the buyer can acknowledge the worthiness of the product,
the result should be a decent livelihood for the one and a
memorable experience for the other. I have been a secretary.
I have been a hustler. Being a hustler is much better for your
self-esteem. I know that for a fact.

JOHN
PRESTON
author

Most of the sex I've seen on the screen looks
like an expression of hostility towards sex.

MYRNA LOY, ACTRESS

Every vice has its excuse ready.

PUBLILIUS SYRUS, GREEK APHORIST

An intellectual is a person who has discovered
something more interesting than sex.

ALDOUS HUXLEY
author, satirist

Never practice two vices at once.

TALLULAH BANKHEAD, ACTRESS

The fear of homosexuality is found in movies more often
than homosexuality itself.

VITO RUSSO, AUTHOR, HISTORIAN, AND ACTIVIST

In America, sex is an obsession;
in other parts of the world it's a fact.

MARLENE DIETRICH, ACTRESS

Humans are the
only animal who
can have sex over
the phone.

DAVID
LETTERMAN
television host

The American ideal of sexuality appears to be rooted in the American ideal of masculinity. This idea has created cowboys and Indians, good guys and bad guys, punks and studs, tough guys and softies, butch and faggot, black and white. It is an ideal so paralytically infantile that it is virtually forbidden—as an unpatriotic act—that the American boy evolve into the complexity of manhood.

JAMES BALDWIN, AUTHOR AND CRITIC

"Without the pioneering pornographers who changed what we thought was indecent, and on rare occasion, subverted artistic lust, I could never have had the nerve to make my movies. Isn't there some sort of Purple Heart for the auteurs of amateur porn? Can't some hotshot university start a Legion of Honor for David Hurles and buy his collection to preserve it forever? The wonderful, terrible, beautifully scary life of David Hurles has been an inspiration to my inner filth for years and it's high time he got the academic respect he so rightfully deserves.

JOHN WATERS, AUTHOR AND FILMMAKER

Heterosexuality is not normal, it's just common.

DOROTHY PARKER
author, satirist

To be yourself in a world that is constantly trying to make you something else is the greatest accomplishment.

RALPH WALDO EMERSON, AUTHOR AND SOCIAL CRITIC

There's only one good test of pornography. Get twelve normal men to read the book, and then ask them, "Did you get an erection?" If the answer is yes from a majority of the twelve, then the book is pornographic.

W.H. AUDEN, AUTHOR

All the things I really like to do are either immoral, illegal, or fattening.

ALEXANDER WOOLLCOTT
humorist

The rules are only barriers to keep the children from falling.

MADAME DE STAEL, AUTHOR

Masturbation: the primary sexual activity of mankind. In the nineteenth century, it was a disease; in the twentieth it's a cure

THOMAS SZASZ, PSYCHIATRIST

Almost everyone has the sexual potential for anything.

KEN LIVINGSTONE
politician

The score never interested me, only the game.

MAE WEST, ACTRESS, FILMMAKER, AND SATIRIST

We are now more sensitive to the reality that race is not a binary question. A root of black ancestry does not make you black, and a strand of same-sex attraction doesn't make you gay. Like racial identity, male sexuality should not be treated as if it were simple as black and white.

MICHAEL LUCAS, PORN FILMMAKER AND ACTIVIST

You cannot blame porn.
When I was young,
I used to masturbate
to *Gilligan's Island.*

RON JEREMY
porn actor

In advertising, sex sells. But only if you're selling sex.

JEF I. RICHARDS, AUTHOR AND EDUCATOR

Pornography is literature designed to be read with one hand.

ANGELA LAMBERT, AUTHOR AND CRITIC

Sadomasochism has always been the furthest reach of the sexual experience: when sex becomes the most purely sexual.

SUSAN SONTAG, AUTHOR, ACTIVIST, AND SOCIAL CRITIC

Nudity is a form of dress.

JOHN BERGER, CRITIC

You have to accept the fact that part of the sizzle of sex comes from the danger of sex. You can be overpowered.

CAMILLE PAGLIA, AUTHOR, EDUCATOR, AND SOCIAL CRITIC

Posing for another picture/Everybody's got to sell/But when you shake your ass/They notice fast/And some mistakes were built to last. ("Freedom 90")

GEORGE MICHAEL, SINGER AND MUSICIAN

Sex and a cocktail: they both lasted about as long, had the same effect, and amounted to about the same thing.

D.H. LAWRENCE
author

Sex is the mysticism of materialism and the only possible religion in a materialistic society.

MALCOLM MUGGERIDGE
author, social critic

There's a tremendous fear of liking sex too much. When we make love, as much as everyone wants to cum and see stars and feel the world turn, we resist intense sexual experience more than we embrace it. And it's very difficult for us to let go. The idea of "letting go" makes people think they're just going to lose it—they won't get up and go to work the next day. I think that sexual repression really is key to the work ethic: the idea that if you pleased your body, you wouldn't be compelled to bring home the bacon, or wax the floor anymore—all those things that you make yourself do because you have to.

SUSIE BRIGHT, AUTHOR AND ACTIVIST

Lord, grant me chastity and continence—but not yet.

ST. AUGUSTINE, THEOLOGIAN

I tend to think that cricket is the greatest thing that God ever created on earth—certainly greater than sex, although sex isn't too bad either.

HAROLD PINTER, DRAMATIST AND NOBEL LAUREATE

We have never heard the devil's side of the story, God wrote all the book.

ANATOLE FRANCE
author

I thank God I was raised Catholic, so sex will always be dirty.

JOHN WATERS, AUTHOR AND FILMMAKER

How can a bishop marry? How can he flirt? The most he can say is, "I will see you in the vestry after service."

SYDNEY SMITH, AUTHOR AND CLERIC

Christianity has enriched the erotic meal with the appetizer of curiosity and spoiled it with the dessert of remorse.

KARL KRAUS, AUTHOR AND SATIRIST

The only time I ask for God's help is when I can't fit it in both my hands.

TRENT ATKINS, PORN ACTOR

To hear many religious people talk,
one would think God created the torso, head, legs,
and arms, but the devil slapped on the genitals.

DON SCHRADER, AUTHOR

Why should we take advice on sex from the Pope? If he knows anything about it, he shouldn't.

GEORGE BERNARD SHAW, PLAYWRIGHT AND JOURNALIST

An erect phallus is a symbol of life, a cross a symbol of death.
(These were Cadinot's final words printed following his death,
per his request.)

JEAN-DANIEL CADINOT, PORN FILMMAKER AND ARTIST

It was the afternoon of my eighty-first birthday, and I was in bed with my catamite when Ali announced that the archbishop had come to see me. (Opening line of *Earthly Powers*)

ANTHONY BURGESS
author, critic

If God had intended us not to masturbate,
he would've made our arms shorter.

GEORGE CARLIN, COMEDIAN AND SOCIAL CRITIC

And it struck me then, that I liked Sean because he looked,
well, slutty. A boy who had been around. A boy who couldn't
remember if he was Catholic or not. (*The Rules of Attraction*)

BRET EASTON ELLIS, AUTHOR

Sex is one of the nine reasons for reincarnation.
The other eight are unimportant.

HENRY MILLER
author, artist

Sex is kicking death in the ass while singing.

CHARLES BUKOWSKI, POET

There are six admonishments in the Bible concerning
homosexual activity—and there are 362 admonishments in the
Bible concerning heterosexual activity. I don't mean to imply by
this that God doesn't love straight people, only that they seem to
require a great deal more supervision.

LYNN LAVNER, COMEDIAN

Fear of sexuality
is the new,
disease~sponsored
register of the
universe of fear in
which everyone
now lives.

SUSAN
SONTAG

author, activist

In all systems of theology the Devil figures as a male person.

DON MARQUIS, HUMORIST AND AUTHOR

Sex is God's joke on human beings.

BETTE
DAVIS

actress

To many, total abstinence is easier than perfect moderation.

ST. AUGUSTINE, THEOLOGIAN

God made him, and therefore let him pass for a man.

(*The Merchant of Venice*)

WILLIAM SHAKESPEARE, PLAYWRIGHT

If God created the body and the body is dirty, then the fault lies
with the manufacturer.

LENNY BRUCE, COMEDIAN AND SATIRIST

Christian: one who follows the teachings of Christ
insofar as they are not inconsistent with a life of sin.

AMBROSE BIERCE, AUTHOR AND SATIRIST

Not every religion has to have St. Augustine's attitude to sex. Why even in our culture marriages are celebrated in a church, everyone present knows what is going to happen that night, but that doesn't prevent it being a religious ceremony.

LUDWIG WITTGENSTEIN, PHILOSOPHER

We've never been intimate.
(On whether God exists.)

NOËL COWARD, DRAMATIST AND WIT

Sex and religion are closer to each other than either might prefer.

THOMAS MORE, STATESMAN AND PHILOSOPHER

Saintliness is also a temptation.
(*Becket*)

JEAN ANOUILH, DRAMATIST

Moral indignation is jealousy with a halo.

H.G. WELLS
author

SEX AND RELIGION

Catholics have more extreme sex lives because they're taught that pleasure is bad for you. Who thinks it's normal to kneel down to a naked man who's nailed to a cross? It's like a bad leather bar.

JOHN WATERS
author, filmmaker

A dead sinner revised and edited.

(On the definition of a saint.)

AMBROSE BIERCE, AUTHOR AND SATIRIST

Christian Fundamentalism: the doctrine that there is an absolutely powerful, infinitely knowledgeable, universe-spanning entity that is deeply and personally concerned about my sex life.

ANDREW LIAS, AUTHOR AND ATHEIST

Of course Heaven forbids certain pleasures, but one finds means of compromise.

MOLIÈRE, PLAYWRIGHT

The only thing wrong with being an atheist is that there's nobody to talk to during an orgasm.

UNKNOWN ORIGIN

Sex touches the heavens only when it simultaneously touches the gutter and the mud.

GEORGE JEAN NATHAN
critic, publisher

Sex is the ersatz or substitute religion of the 20th century.

MALCOLM MUGGERIDGE, AUTHOR AND SOCIAL CRITIC

The strongest, surest way to the soul is through the flesh.

MABEL
DODGE LUHAN

heiress, arts patron

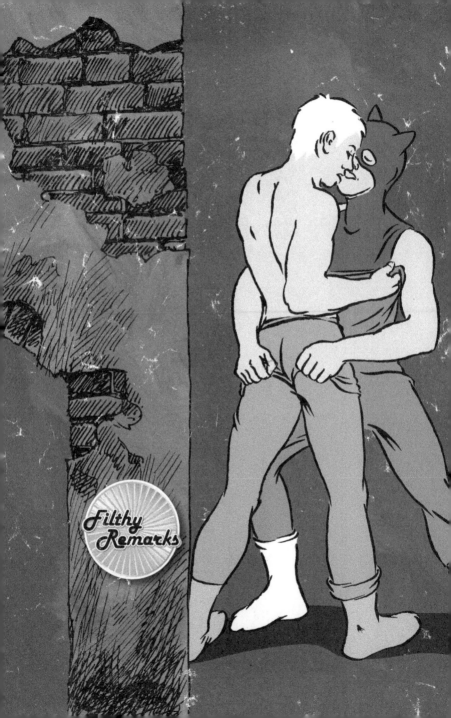

Every man has a wild animal in him.

FREDERICK
THE GREAT
military leader

I need to cum. I need to. Cumming is a need. I came the first
time when I was 12 and I haven't skipped a day. I cum every
day—and I've fucked maybe 20 times in my life. So it's just
been me doing most of the work.

LOUIS C.K., COMEDIAN

Though we adore men individually, we agree that as a group
they're rather stupid.
("Sister Suffragette" from *Mary Poppins*)

SHERMAN BROTHERS, SONGWRITERS

Years ago, manhood was an opportunity for achievement, and
now it is a problem to be overcome.

GARRISON KEILLOR, AUTHOR AND HUMORIST

Let my lusts be my ruin, then,
since all else is a fake and a mockery.

HART CRANE, POET

Men do not change; they unmask themselves.

MADAME DE STAEL, AUTHOR

There is probably no sensitive heterosexual alive who is not
preoccupied with his latent homosexuality.

NORMAN MAILER, AUTHOR

Men don't fake orgasm—no man wants to pull a face like that
on purpose.

ALLAN
PEASE

author

Where's the man could ease a heart like a satin gown?

DOROTHY PARKER, AUTHOR AND SATIRIST

A man's kiss is his signature.

MAE WEST, ACTRESS, FILMMAKER, AND SATIRIST

Loosen up. Being masculine doesn't mean being a statue.
Wrists were made to bend.

KEN
HANES

author

A gentleman is simply a patient wolf.

LANA TURNER, ACTRESS

Men are so made that they can resist sound argument,
and yet yield to a glance.

HONORÉ DE BALZAC, DRAMATIST

The perfect lover is one who turns into a pizza at 4:00 a.m.

CHARLES PIERCE, PERFORMER AND HUMORIST

It's one thing to shoot a man, quite another to cast aspersions
upon his lovemaking skills.

TERESA MEDEIROS, AUTHOR

There's very little advice in men's magazines, because men
think, "I know what I'm doing. Just show me somebody naked."

JERRY SEINFELD, COMEDIAN

It's not the men in my life that counts—it's the life in my men.

MAE WEST, ACTRESS, FILMMAKER, AND SATIRIST

See, the problem is that God gives men a brain and a penis, and
only enough blood to run one at a time.

ROBIN WILLIAMS, COMEDIAN

Fifty percent of life in the N.B.A. is sex. The other fifty percent is money.

DENNIS RODMAN

basketball player

I love men like some people love good food or wine.

GERMAINE GREER, AUTHOR AND ACTIVIST

Most men do not mature, they simply grow taller.

LEO ROSTEN, HUMORIST AND EDUCATOR

For the record, I know I am not a reformed character and
I'm not ashamed of my life so far. I know I'm odd—and that
ultimately the joke's on me.

AIDEN
SHAW
porn actor, author

Understand that sexuality is as wide as the sea. Understand
that your morality is not law. Understand that we are you.
Understand that if we decide to have sex whether safe, safer
or unsafe, it is our decision and you have no rights in our
lovemaking.

DEREK JARMAN, FILMMAKER

Macho does not prove mucho.

ZSA ZSA
GABOR
socialite

An orgasm joins you to the past. Its timelessness becomes the brotherhood; the brethren are lovers; they extend the "family." I share that sexuality. It was then, is now and will be in the future.

DEREK JARMAN, FILMMAKER

We have reason to believe that man first walked upright to free his hands for masturbation.

LILY TOMLIN, COMEDIAN

To hear two American men congratulating each other on being heterosexual is one of the most chilling experiences—and unique to the United States. You don't hear two Italians sitting around complimenting each other because they actually like to go to bed with women. The American is hysterical about his manhood.

GORE VIDAL, AUTHOR

Man is Nature's sole mistake.

W.S. GILBERT, DRAMATIST AND ILLUSTRATOR

As long as you know that most men are like children, you know everything.

COCO CHANEL, FASHION DESIGNER AND ARTIST

I never resist temptation, because I have found that the things
that are bad for me do not tempt me.

GEORGE
BERNARD SHAW
playwright, journalist

The more I see of men, the more I like dogs.

MADAME DE STAEL, AUTHOR

Honesty. If that doesn't work, try horse tranquilizers, or money.
(On how he can be seduced.)

STEVE O'DONNELL, PORN ACTOR

Don't be indirect with men. Men are stupid.

DAN SAVAGE, SEX COLUMNIST AND ACTIVIST

I wouldn't recommend sex, drugs, or insanity for everyone,
but they've always worked for me.

HUNTER S. THOMPSON, AUTHOR AND HUMORIST

An improper mind is a perpetual feast.

LOGAN PEARSALL SMITH, ESSAYIST AND CRITIC

I want a man who's kind and understanding. Is that too much
to ask of a millionaire?

Zsa Zsa Gabor, socialite

I don't pay them for sex. I pay them to leave.
(on hiring prostitutes)

Charlie Sheen, actor

Of the delights of this world, man cares most for sexual
intercourse. He will go to any length for it—risk fortune,
character, reputation, life itself. And what do you think he has
done? He has left it out of his Heaven! Prayer takes its place.

Every man over forty is a scoundrel.

George Bernard Shaw, playwright and journalist

A man has missed something if he has never woken up in an
anonymous bed beside a face he'll never see again, and if he
has never left a brothel at dawn feeling like throwing himself
into the river out of sheer disgust with life.

Gustave Flaubert, author

JAYNE
MANSFIELD

actress, beauty icon

SEX AND MEN

Men are those creatures with two legs and eight hands.

There are three kinds of men. The one that learns by reading. The few who learn by observation. The rest of them have to pee on the electric fence for themselves.

WILL ROGERS performer, humorist

Women need a reason to have sex. Men just need a place.

BILLY CRYSTAL, COMEDIAN

I only like two kinds of men—domestic and imported.

MAE WEST, ACTRESS, FILMMAKER, AND SATIRIST

I love the smell of a man. I hate colognes, I hate deodorants. If someone's wearing cologne, I don't care how attractive he is—I won't have anything to do with him! Cologne gives me a headache. And there's nothing worse than licking someone's armpit and tasting deodorant. As much as my boyfriend loves how I smell, he was just telling me, 'You've got to take a shower today, man! You stink!' But I told him that I love being able to smell myself as I'm walking through the room.

MAX STONE, PORN ACTOR

I like men who have a future and women who have a past.

OSCAR WILDE, AUTHOR AND WIT

Anybody who believes that the way to a man's heart is through his stomach flunked geography.

ROBERT BYRNE, AUTHOR

Men are beasts and even beasts don't behave as they do.

BRIGITTE BARDOT, ACTRESS AND BEAUTY ICON

For sheer sexiness, a man must be beautiful. Funny, yes. Clever, no.

JILLY COOPER, author

I love men, even though they're lying, cheating scumbags.

GWYNETH PALTROW, ACTRESS

Straight men would do everything gay men do if straight men could but straight men can't because straight women won't.

DAN SAVAGE, SEX COLUMNIST AND ACTIVIST

I don't know the question, but sex is definitely the answer.

WOODY ALLEN, FILMMAKER

Sex is work.

ANDY WARHOL, ARTIST AND FILMMAKER

I made love and was happy.

JOSEPH ADDISON, AUTHOR AND POLITICIAN

There is nothing wrong with going to bed with someone of your own sex. People should be very free with sex, but they should draw the line at goats.

ELTON JOHN
singer, musician

I don't like her—but don't misunderstand me: my dislike is purely platonic.

HERBERT BEERBOHM TREE, ACTOR

Sex: the thing that takes up the least amount of time and causes the most amount of trouble.

JOHN BARRYMORE, ACTOR

Sex and beauty are inseparable, like life and consciousness. And the intelligence which goes with sex and beauty, and arises out of sex and beauty, is intuition.

D.H. LAWRENCE
author

Love is not the dying moan of a distant violin—it's the triumphant twang of a bedspring.

S.J. PERELMAN, HUMORIST

The difference between light and hard is that you can sleep with a light on.

UNKNOWN ORIGIN

Remember, if you smoke after sex you're doing it too fast.

WOODY ALLEN, FILMMAKER

The important thing in acting is to laugh and cry.
If I have to cry, I think of my sex life.
If I have to laugh, I think of my sex life.

GLENDA JACKSON
actress, politician

What arouses me most is when I'm fucking somebody, to see that I really, really, really arouse them. The more they are screaming, the more I see that I'm doing very well, the more hot it is for me. I really love to fuck very hard and it doesn't matter if it is boy or girl. We say in Europe, "They can't be dead in bed." They must respond. So, if they respond—and how they respond—that's what interests me.

DANO SULIK, PORN ACTOR

We think about sex obsessively except during the act, when our minds tend to wander.

HOWARD NEMEROV, POET

While having sex, I like to watch my partner's face. Watching their faces gets me off big time. You watch their face and you see them really getting off on what you're doing to them. That's how you find out if you're a good lover.

VINCE ROCKLAND, PORN ACTOR

Sex without love is a meaningless experience, but as far as meaningless experiences go it's pretty damn good.

WOODY ALLEN
filmmaker

A narcissist is someone better-looking than you are.

GORE VIDAL, AUTHOR

If you go home with somebody, and they don't have books,
don't fuck them!

JOHN WATERS, AUTHOR AND FILMMAKER

My own belief is that there is hardly anyone whose sexual
life, if it were broadcast, would not fill the world at large with
surprise and horror.

W. SOMERSET MAUGHAM, author

Whoever called it necking was a poor judge of anatomy.

GROUCHO MARX, ACTOR AND SATIRIST

Everything you see I owe to spaghetti.

SOPHIA LOREN, ACTRESS AND BEAUTY ICON

The good thing about masturbation is that you don't have to get
dressed up for it.

TRUMAN CAPOTE, AUTHOR AND HUMORIST

Graze on my lips;
and if those hills
be dry, stray lower,
where the pleasant
fountains lie...
("Venus and Adonis")

WILLIAM
SHAKESPEARE
playwright

It's okay to laugh in the bedroom as long as you don't point.

WILL DURST, comedian

Kids. They're not easy. But there has to be some penalty for sex.

BILL MAHER, COMEDIAN AND SOCIAL CRITIC

Beyond the beauty, the sex, the titillation, the surface,
there is a human being. And that has to emerge.

JEANNE MOREAU, ACTRESS AND BEAUTY ICON

Don't marry someone you would not be friends with
if there was no sex between you.

WILLIAM GLASSER, PSYCHIATRIST

Sex without love has its place, and it's pretty cool, but when
you have it hand-in-hand with deep commitment and respect
and caring, it's nine-thousand times better.

GEORGE CARLIN, COMEDIAN AND SOCIAL CRITIC

Normal people have sex lives of their own to worry about.

JESSICA CUTLER, BLOGGER AND SEX WRITER

The real way to avoid HIV is not by avoiding people
with HIV; it's by avoiding practices that make HIV
communicable. If you want to stay negative,
assume that everyone you hook up with is positive,
and wear a condom to protect yourself. If the relationship
moves beyond sex, there will be a time when it's appropriate
to talk about your medical histories. That may mean
continuing to practice safe sex—but if you love a guy, a thin
layer of rubber shouldn't be enough to keep you apart.
Until then, it's none of your business.

MICHAEL
LUCAS
porn filmmaker

Sex is a two-way treat.

FRANKLIN P. JONES, HUMORIST

It was all oddly innocent and joyful for me.
The main thrill was just knowing I was out there turning on
men on TVs across the world. That's a thrill as an actor and
also as an exhibitionist. I like the idea of people getting off on
me and the idea of people getting off period.

SCOTT O'HARA, PORN ACTOR, AUTHOR, AND ACTIVIST

The storm caused by our god, sex, sends us all
to our ruin by the shortest route.

ELFRIEDE JELINEK, AUTHOR

Truth is revealed in bed.

JOHANN LOUW, ARTIST

Sex is like snow, you never know how many inches you're going
to get or how long it will last.

UNKNOWN ORIGIN

Love is the answer, but while you are waiting for the answer,
sex raises some pretty good questions.

WOODY ALLEN, FILMMAKER

We settle for so-so sex because most of us don't know how
sexual we could be; we know only how sexual we are. How
sexual we are has been shaped by decades of indoctrination by
family and friends, teachers, religious leaders, and romantic
partners, not to mention a society that worships a bewildering
fusion of childlike sexual innocence and cynical, nihilistic
hedonism… So what is normal?
It all depends on what's normal for you.

ANITA H. CLAYTON, AUTHOR

I think anything that has to do with sexuality makes people
very interested.

CATHERINE DENEUVE, ACTRESS AND BEAUTY ICON

Lovemaking seems all too absurd when described.

DAN
SIMMONS
author

Love's mysteries in souls do grow/But yet the body is his book.

JOHN DONNE, POET

There's nothing inherently dirty about sex, but if you try real
hard and use your imagination you can overcome that.

LEWIS GRIZZARD, COMEDIAN

I was like, "Am I gay? Am I straight?"
And I realized, I'm just slutty. Where's my parade?

MARGARET CHO, COMEDIAN AND ACTIVIST

I don't see so much of Alfred anymore
since he got so interested in sex.

MRS. ALFRED KINSEY, RESEARCHER

Sex is
the biggest
nothing
of all time.

ANDY
WARHOL

artist, filmmaker

I think everyone really is bi.

I think everyone will be turned on to the sex they're not normally turned on to at some point in their life.

If you're the gayest guy in the whole world, you will be turned on to some woman. Whether you have sex with her or not, it doesn't depend on that. Likewise, if you're the straightest guy in the world, you may be turned on by a really hot guy. Again, it doesn't matter whether you have sex with him or not.

Now, personally, I think that people should go ahead and do their stuff if they feel like they want to.

It gets it out there in the open. It lets them know if they really like it.

It lets them know what their feelings are.

VINCE ROCKLAND
porn actor

Sex is the most fun you can have without laughing.

WOODY ALLEN, FILMMAKER

Sexual intercourse is a slight attack of apoplexy.

DEMOCRITUS, GREEK PHILOSOPHER

Sex: the pleasure is momentary, the position ridiculous,

and the expense damnable.

LORD CHESTERFIELD, STATESMAN

Remember, sex is like a Chinese dinner.

It ain't over 'til you both get your cookie.

ALEC BALDWIN
actor

While a person does not give up on sex,

sex does not give up on the person.

GABRIEL GARCIA MÁRQUEZ, AUTHOR AND NOBEL LAUREATE

Forget health clinics and gyms. Sex is the best cure. One good

night of sex and your problems are gone.

GRACE JONES, PERFORMER

I swear, people don't want sex so much as

they want somebody who'll listen to them. The first thing you

learn after fellatio is how to listen.

JANE WAGNER, AUTHOR AND COMEDIAN

The only
unnatural sex act
is that which you
cannot perform.

ALFRED
KINSEY
researcher, author

There is nothing safe about sex. There never will be.

NORMAN MAILER, AUTHOR

Love ain't nothing but sex misspelled.

HARLAN ELLISON, AUTHOR

I'm a simple dirty girl who loves a good steak,
a good fuck, and to make people laugh.
Number one is to make people laugh.
Then a good steak, then a good fuck.
Interview any famous conductor at Carnegie Hall,
and they'd say the same thing. They'd like a good
pointer or some good sheet music and a good fuck.

KATHY GRIFFIN, COMEDIAN

Everybody loves you when they are about to cum.

(*Sex*)

I really think that sex always looks kind of funny in a movie.

WILLIAM FRIEDKIN, FILMMAKER

Of all sexual aberrations, chastity is the strangest.

ANATOLE FRANCE, AUTHOR

The big difference between sex
for money and sex for free is that sex for money
usually costs a lot less.

BRENDAN BEHAN, AUTHOR

If you are incapable of a monogamous commitment, don't
make one… The other thing that really helps with a successful
open relationship is a long period of sexual exclusivity at the
start. I think when you prove to each other that you don't
need anyone else, actually having somebody else every once
in awhile is less of a threat… When gay guys say something
like that people expect all sorts of horrible things: slings over
the dining room table with goats under it. And "openness" can
mean open like the Great Plains, or it can mean the door open
a crack. But you have to negotiate that. And the best place to
negotiate that from is a place of serenity and strength, where
you're at peace with each other and secure in your
relationship and really secure with your sexual
bond with each other, and your emotional bond.
And you can't be at that place in two months.

DAN SAVAGE, SEX COLUMNIST AND ACTIVIST

I need sex for a clear complexion but I'd rather do it for love.

JOAN CRAWFORD, ACTRESS

I started to be really proud of the fact I was gay
even though I wasn't.

KURT COBAIN
singer, songwriter

'Tisn't beauty, so to speak, nor a good talk, necessarily.
It's just It. (*Traffics and Discoveries*)

RUDYARD KIPLING, AUTHOR

Give your erotic identity the benefit of your admiration.

SUSIE BRIGHT, AUTHOR AND ACTIVIST

Kinky is using a feather. Perverted is using the whole chicken.

UNKNOWN ORIGIN

I think that one should view with philosophic admiration
the strange paths of the libido and should investigate the
purposes of its circuitous ways.

CARL JUNG, PSYCHOLOGIST

I like someone who is a little crazy but coming from a good place. I think scars are sexy because it means you made a mistake that led to a mess.

ANGELINA
JOLIE

actress

We have big brains and we're kind of endlessly perverse and whatever there is out there in the world somebody is perving out to it. And we should just stand back in awe of our capacity to eroticize just about anything and not question other people's kinks or turn-ons—too much. Just enjoy.

DAN SAVAGE, SEX COLUMNIST AND ACTIVIST

But did thee feel the earth move?
(*For Whom the Bell Tolls*)

ERNEST
HEMINGWAY
author

More than two shakes and it's playing with yourself.

HOMER SIMPSON, CARTOON DAD

I don't like threeways. I've had a few. I don't enjoy them. They make me feel like a competitive eater.

MARGARET CHO, COMEDIAN AND ACTIVIST

Sex is identical to comedy in that it involves timing.

PHYLLIS DILLER, COMEDIAN

We are burdened with assumptions that sex is the dirtiest thing you can do. People go miles out of their way to defend their artistic and intellectual ambitions by saying, "This work is not about sex." That's how you're supposed to be able to tell how grand and incredible it is—that it's not sexual.

SUSIE BRIGHT
author, activist

Sex is like having dinner: sometimes you joke about the dishes, sometimes you take the meal seriously.

WOODY ALLEN, FILMMAKER

Sex—or lack thereof—is at the center of everyone's identity, and once you've cracked someone's desires, you understand them in full.

ARIANNE COHEN, HUMORIST

Those who have great passions find themselves all their lives both happy and unhappy at being cured of them.

FRANÇOIS DE LA ROCHEFOUCAULD, AUTHOR AND APHORIST

Litigation takes the place of sex at middle age.

GORE VIDAL, AUTHOR

Is life not a hundred times too short for us to stifle ourselves?

FRIEDRICH NIETZSCHE
philosopher

Sex is a bad thing because it rumples the clothes.

JACKIE KENNEDY, former first lady

A man marries to have a home,
but also because he doesn't want to be bothered
with sex and all that sort of thing.

W. SOMERSET MAUGHAM, AUTHOR

Desperate is not a sexual preference.

RANDY MILHOLLAND, CARTOONIST AND AUTHOR

The reluctance to osculate has to do with affection—the idea
that we'll blow someone because we desire him, but kiss him
because we like him.

SIMON SHEPPARD, AUTHOR

I don't want to see the uncut version of anything.

JEAN KERR, PLAYWRIGHT

Good dick will make you sign a blank check.

MICHAEL K., GOSSIP BLOGGER

A kiss may ruin a human life.

OSCAR WILDE, AUTHOR AND WIT

Electric flesh-arrows…traversing the body.
A rainbow of color strikes the eyelids. A foam of music falls
over the ears. It is the gong of the orgasm.

ANAÏS
NIN

author, lover

Once you see your nature, sex is basically immaterial.

BODHIDHARMA, BUDDHIST MONK

Tell him I've been too fucking busy—or vice versa.

DOROTHY PARKER, AUTHOR AND SATIRIST

A really hard laugh is like sex—one of the ultimate diversions
of existence.

JERRY SEINFELD, COMEDIAN

The only way to get rid of a temptation is to yield to it.

OSCAR WILDE, AUTHOR AND WIT

The butt is not a magical place that only gay people can visit,
like a leather bar or the Liberace Museum.

DAN SAVAGE, SEX COLUMNIST AND ACTIVIST

When you make love you're using up energy;
and afterwards you feel happy and don't give
a damn for anything. They can't bear you to feel
like that. They want you to be bursting with energy
all the time. All this marching up and down and
cheering and waving flags is simply sex gone sour.
If you're happy inside yourself, why should you
get excited about Big Brother and the Three-Year
Plans and the Two Minutes Hate and all
the rest of their bloody rot?

(*1984*)

GEORGE
ORWELL
author, activist

Sex is full of lies. The body tries to tell the truth. But, it's usually
too battered with rules to be heard, and bound with pretenses
so it can hardly move. We cripple ourselves with lies.

JIM MORRISON, SINGER AND ARTIST

Sex between two people is a beautiful thing;
between five it's fantastic.

WOODY ALLEN, FILMMAKER

If we resist our passions, it is due more to their weakness
than our own strength.

FRANÇOIS DE LA ROCHEFOUCAULD, AUTHOR AND APHORIST

I'm all for bringing back the birch,
but only between consenting adults.

GORE VIDAL, AUTHOR

Yes, exercise is the catalyst. That's what makes everything
happen: your digestion, your elimination, your sex life, your
skin, hair, everything about you depends on circulation. And
how do you increase circulation?

JACK LALANNE, FITNESS GURU

Sex is like money; only too much is enough.

JOHN
UPDIKE

author

If people will stop at the first tense of the verb "aimer"
they must not be surprised if one finishes
the conjugation with somebody else.

LORD BYRON, POET AND LOVER

The only difference between friends and lovers is about four
minutes.

SCOTT ROEBEN, HUMORIST

In my sex fantasy, nobody ever loves me for my mind.

NORA EPHRON, FILMMAKER AND HUMORIST

Nothing risqué, nothing gained.

ALEXANDER WOOLLCOTT, HUMORIST

If sex is such a natural phenomenon,
how come there are so many books on how to do it?

BETTE
MIDLER
singer, actor

Pleasure is more trouble than trouble.

DON HEROLD, HUMORIST

Seduction is always more singular and sublime than sex and it commands the higher price.

JEAN BAUDRILLARD, ARTIST AND PHILOSOPHER

I want a man, not a boy who thinks he can.

("2 Become 1")

SPICE GIRLS
singers

Home is heaven and orgies are vile/

But you need an orgy, once in awhile.

OGDEN NASH, POET AND HUMORIST

Certainly nothing is unnatural that is not physically impossible.

RICHARD SHERIDAN, PLAYWRIGHT AND POET

After coition, every animal is sad.

UNKNOWN ORIGIN

When people say, "You're breaking my heart," they do in fact usually mean that you're breaking their genitals.

JEFFREY BERNARD, JOURNALIST

No matter how much cats fight, there always seem to be plenty of kittens.

ABRAHAM
LINCOLN
16th U.S. president

Is that a gun in your pocket,

or are you just happy to see me?

Mae West, actress, filmmaker, and satirist

When I have sex with someone

I forget who I am.

For a minute I even forget I'm human.

It's the same thing when I'm behind a camera.

I forget I exist.

ROBERT MAPPLETHORPE
artist

A chicken and an egg are lying in bed.

The chicken is smoking a cigarette with

a satisfied smile on its face and the egg

is frowning and looking put out. The egg mutters,

"I guess we answered that question."

UNKNOWN ORIGIN

Do anything, but let it produce joy.

Do anything, but let it yield ecstasy.

Henry Miller, author and artist

Sex alleviates tension. Love causes it.

WOODY ALLEN
filmmaker

Blake said that the body was the soul's prison unless the five senses are fully developed and open. He considered the senses the "windows of the soul." When sex involves all the senses intensely, it can be like a mystical experience.

JIM MORRISON
singer, artist

Once you've gotten two hands up somebody's ass, you aren't likely to feel jealous of a penis.

PATRICK CALIFIA, TRANS ACTIVIST AND AUTHOR

If you don't believe in oral sex, keep your mouth shut.

UNKNOWN ORIGIN

Sex is the great amateur art.

DAVID CORT, AUTHOR

It is not sex that gives the pleasure, but the lover.

MARGE PIERCY, AUTHOR

Sex is like art. Most of it is pretty bad,
and the good stuff is out of your price range.

SCOTT ROEBEN, HUMORIST

Your idea of fidelity
is not having more than one man
in bed at the same time. (*Darling*)

FREDERIC RAPHAEL, DRAMATIST AND AUTHOR

Having sex is like playing bridge. If you don't have a good
partner, you'd better have a good hand.

WOODY ALLEN, FILMMAKER

The thing about sex is no matter
how much you crave it, you can forget it.

CHUCK PALAHNIUK, AUTHOR

Sex appeal is fifty percent
what you've got and fifty percent
what people think you've got.

SOPHIA
LOREN
actress, beauty icon

Sex at age 90 is like trying to shoot pool with a rope.

GEORGE BURNS, COMEDIAN

Sex got me into trouble from the age of fifteen.
I'm hoping that by the time I'm seventy I'll straighten it out.

HAROLD ROBBINS, AUTHOR

If someone had told me years ago that sharing
a sense of humour was so vital to partnerships,
I could have avoided a lot of sex.

KATE BECKINSALE, ACTRESS

The real tragedy is when you've got sex in the head
instead of down where it belongs.

D.H.
LAWRENCE
author, critic

My candle burns at both ends;
It will not last the night;
But ah, my foes, and oh, my friends—
It gives a lovely light!

EDNA ST. VINCENT MILLAY, POET AND PLAYWRIGHT

Sex lies at the root of life, and we can never learn to reverence
life until we know how to understand sex.

HENRY HAVELOCK ELLIS, SEXOLOGIST

If sex doesn't scare the cat, you're not doing it right.

Sex is hardly ever just about sex.

SHIRLEY MACLAINE
actress, author

Sex is a conversation carried out by other means. If you get on well out of bed, half the problems of bed are solved.

PETER USTINOV, ACTOR

Of all the animals on earth, none is so brutish as man when he seeks the delirium of coition.

EDWARD DAHLBERG
author

Commit/The oldest sins the newest kind of ways.

(Henry IV, Part II)

WILLIAM SHAKESPEARE, PLAYWRIGHT

Homosexuality is regarded
as shameful by barbarians and by those who live
under despotic governments just as philosophy is regarded as
shameful by them, because it is apparently not in
the interest of such rulers to have great ideas engendered
in their subjects, or powerful friendships or passionate
love—all of which homosexuality is particularly
apt to produce.

PLATO, GREEK PHILOSOPHER

Surely the sex business isn't worth all this damned fuss? I've
met only a handful of people who cared a biscuit for it.

T.E. LAWRENCE, MILITARY OFFICER AND AUTHOR

The louder he talked of his honor,
the faster we counted our spoons.

RALPH WALDO EMERSON
author, social critic

Come live with me and be my love

And we will all the pleasures prove...

CHRISTOPHER MARLOWE, POET

I can remember when the air was clean and sex was dirty.

GEORGE
BURNS
comedian

It's an old complaint that our language doesn't have the nuance
and variety to convey the sexual experience. It's a complaint
based on laziness and prudishness—English is a fine language
to fuck with.

SUSIE BRIGHT, AUTHOR AND ACTIVIST

If your life at night is good, you think you have everything.

EURIPIDES, GREEK DRAMATIST

For thirty years I served her Majesty at home and abroad
without acknowledgment or reward. Then I publish a
pornographic book, and at once earn £10,000 and fame. I
begin at last to understand the public and what it wants.

SIR RICHARD FRANCIS BURTON, EXPLORER AND AUTHOR

Pleasure is the only thing to live for. Nothing ages like happiness.

OSCAR WILDE
author, wit

It's a bawdy planet.

(*The Winter's Tale*)

WILLIAM SHAKESPEARE, PLAYWRIGHT

One half of the world cannot understand
the pleasures of the other.

JANE AUSTEN, AUTHOR

The very general occurrence of the homosexual in ancient
Greece, and its wide occurrence today in some cultures in
which such activity is not taboo suggests that the capacity of an
individual to respond erotically to any sort of stimulus, whether
it is provided by another person of the same or opposite sex, is
basic in the species.

ALFRED KINSEY, BIOLOGIST, RESEARCHER, AND AUTHOR

Just because society, and government, and whatever was
different 100 years ago, doesn't mean that people didn't have
sex, pick their nose, or swear.

KATE WINSLET, ACTRESS

I think it is funny that we were freer about sexuality
in the 4th century BC. It is a little disconcerting.

ANGELINA JOLIE, ACTRESS

Gay men are the guardians
of the masculine impulse. To have
Anonymous sex in a dark alleyway
is to pay homage to the dream
of male freedom. The unknown stranger is
a wandering pagan god. The altar, as in
pre-history, is anywhere you kneel.

CAMILLE PAGLIA, AUTHOR, EDUCATOR, AND SOCIAL CRITIC

Literature is all, or mostly, about sex.

ANTHONY BURGESS, AUTHOR AND CRITIC

Nope, no sex scandals yet.
But I am open to offers!

Zeus performed acts with swans and heifers
that would debar him from every London club
except the Garrick or possibly
the Naval and Military.

STEPHEN FRY, AUTHOR AND ACTOR

For to tempt and to be tempted are things very nearly allied, and in spite of the finest maxims of morality impressed on the mind, whenever feeling has anything to do in the matter, no sooner is it excited than we have already gone vastly farther than we are aware of.

CATHERINE THE GREAT

empress of Russia

Everything in the world is about sex except sex.

Sex is about power.

OSCAR WILDE, AUTHOR AND WIT

One of the things being in politics has taught me is that men
are not a reasoned or reasonable sex.

MARGARET
THATCHER

former UK, premier

My first time I jacked off, I thought I'd invented it.

I looked down at my sloppy handful of junk and thought:

This is going to make me rich.

CHUCK PALAHNIUK, AUTHOR

Republicans sleep in twin beds—some even in separate rooms.

That is why there are more Democrats.

UNKNOWN ORIGIN

Sex is an activity. Pornography is an attitude toward that
activity.

ROGER
EBERT

film critic, author

One man's blasphemy doesn't override other people's free-speech rights, their freedom to publish, freedom of thought.

DAN SAVAGE, SEX COLUMNIST AND ACTIVIST

An orgy looks particularly alluring seen through the mists of righteous indignation.

MALCOLM MUGGERIDGE, AUTHOR AND SOCIAL CRITIC

How did sex come to be thought of as dirty in the first place? God must have been a Republican.

WILL DURST, COMEDIAN

It depends on what the meaning of the word "is" is.
(During grand jury testimony on his affair with Monica Lewinsky)

BILL CLINTON
42nd U.S. president

Republican boys date Democratic girls.
They plan to marry Republican girls, but feel they're entitled to a little fun first.

UNKNOWN ORIGIN

Clinton lied.
A man might forget where
he parks or where he
lives, but he never forgets
oral sex, no matter how
bad it is.

BARBARA
BUSH
former first lady

Men are more easily governed through their vices
than through their virtues.

NAPOLEON BONAPARTE, military leader

Sex is the last refuge of the miserable.

QUENTIN CRISP, AUTHOR AND HUMORIST

They don't call me Tyrannosaurus Sex for nothing.

TED KENNEDY, U.S. SENATOR FROM MASSACHUSETTS

Conservatives say teaching sex education in the public schools
will promote promiscuity. With our education system? If
we promote promiscuity the same way we promote math or
science, they've got nothing to worry about.

BEVERLY MICKINS, AUTHOR AND ACTIVIST

Fighting for peace is like screwing for virginity.

GEORGE CARLIN, COMEDIAN AND SOCIAL CRITIC

Why do Republicans hate gay marriage so much?
They certainly don't hate gay prostitutes.

MARGARET CHO, COMEDIAN AND ACTIVIST

The people do not mind fornication but they loathe adultery.

RAMSAY MACDONALD, FORMER PRIME MINISTER OF THE UK

Politics is supposed to be the second-oldest profession.
I have come to realize that it bears a very close resemblance
to the first.

RONALD REAGAN
40th U.S. president

Men chase by night those they will not greet by day.

CAMILLE PAGLIA, AUTHOR, EDUCATOR, AND SOCIAL CRITIC

"Obscenity" is whatever gives the judge an erection.

UNKNOWN ORIGIN

Sex is on the minds of most people,
especially those who shouldn't be having it.

WILLIAM GLASSER, PSYCHIATRIST

Obscenity is such a tiny kingdom that a single tour covers it
completely.

HEYWOOD BROUN, AUTHOR AND ACTIVIST

The difference between pornography and erotica is lighting.

GLORIA
LEONARD
porn actor, activist

Every single person who has criticized the porn
I make is laboring under a misunderstanding of
what porn is. Hundreds of serious academics and
governmental studies have shown that porn—if it is good
porn—functions as a cathartic agent that relieves pent-up
sexual energy. It's been shown over and over that porn doesn't
lead to any particular kind of behavior, whether it's violent
or unsafe. Rather, it allows the viewer to live the experience
vicariously, to be free from the need or the drive to act unwisely
or uncharacteristically. The most famous porn studies from
around the world show that cultures that have the most
graphic and honest and freely available pornography are
also the cultures with the healthiest sexuality. Porn is like any
of the arts: to function correctly and healthily it has
to be honest and it has to be fearless.

PAUL
MORRIS
porn filmmaker

I write pornography because it is a form of gay men's vernacular literature. It is created in our own language about our own passions and the ways we use our bodies to express those passions. If another person can get beyond his or her prejudices to be able to hear the beauty in pornography or listen to its truths, they are welcome, but the purpose of pornography is not to win endorsement. Nor should gay art be an attempt at sympathy or approval. Gay art of all kinds should be a statement of being. The response of any group or organization that claims inclusivity must be to work to acknowledge these statements.

JOHN PRESTON
author

Pornography is in the loin of the beholder.

CHARLES REMBAR, LAWYER

To be honest, I probably have more sex in the videos than I do in my private life. I know that most people wouldn't believe that. They tend to think, Oh, you're a porn star, so you must be a complete slut! And with a lot of people, it's true. But there are quite a lot of us who don't fit that image.

TOM KATT, PORN ACTOR

People get hysterical about sex.

They want pornography to do the job that they themselves are not doing, which is educating our young people how to be safer. Unless a pornography movie is advertised as educational, it is not educational. And the fact that people are reduced to looking at an entertainment medium to find out about sex is sad. It would be less sad if it wasn't so tragic. Watching pornography to find out about how sex works is like watching a James Bond movie to find out how spies do their job.

NINA HARTLEY, PORN ACTRESS AND ACTIVIST

All history is pornography.

FRANCESCA DA RIMINI
artist

At some point I got so tired of being told that I had to present sex in a certain way: shaved musclemen wearing condoms, posing just so, talking pathetic porntalk. None of the guys who were having sex for my cameras were wearing condoms or acting like porn mannequins during their actual sex, and at some point I just decided to start my own company and make porn honestly. Sex is much too important to lie about.

PAUL MORRIS, PORN FILMMAKER AND SOCIAL CRITIC

All my life is one big fuck!

I have been shooting porn all of my adult life.

Sometimes, when I am having sex with my wife,

I give her direction. I tell her, "Hold it like this.

Turn it this way." And she will say to me, "No.

We are not on camera." But my friends now

all know what I do and they do not care

about it. This is different from when I was younger.

Now, I go home to my family and leave my

thoughts about working here in the office.

MARTY STEVENS, ADULT FILMMAKER

A lof of people don't understand

that adult film isn't about attraction and arousal;

it's about getting a hard-on on cue.

I'd use an acting technique—it's like a playback

method in your mind. I would concentrate

on something that really turned me on—something

I'd either seen, touched, smelled, tasted, whatever

gave me that charge. That's how I got hard.

REX
CHANDLER
porn actor

There's a subterranean impetus towards pornography so powerful that half the business world is juiced by the sort of halfsex that one finds in advertisements.

NORMAN MAILER
author

SEX AND PORNOGRAPHY

One of the things that I didn't figure in doing porn was that people were going to have such vehemently negative feelings about it. I've gotten emails from people saying that it's abhorrent and that it goes against what's right and normal. And these are people in my own community. You know, I still think we're dealing with a lot of shame in our community. There are people who really get into porn and then lash out against guys who do the films. I guess they don't feel entitled to enjoy that sexual part of themselves. I will say, however, that there are plenty of people who are more than able to look beyond that part of my career to see what else I have to offer. Those are the people I'm looking to reach.

COLTON FORD
porn actor, singer

If you are doing your work you're completely focused and really don't think all about the [activity] going on around you. I think, for me, it's those hurry-up-and-wait moments on the set when I'm sitting there just stroking it, keeping it good and hard for the next shot, when it suddenly dawns on me that everyone is just doing their job, and mine is exactly this.

It can be a little surreal.

MATT SIZEMORE, PORN ACTOR

Not everybody can be a porn star.

You can be a porn participant.

But one job and you're a porn star?

I don't think so.

HEATHER McDONALD, COMEDIAN

Porn stars and drag queens were never in the closet. We were
always brave and out there because, yes, it is brave to be a drag
queen, and you have to have guts to be in porn in our society.
It's the nonhomogenized part of our movement that keeps
LGBT culture alive.

MICHAEL LUCAS, PORN FILMMAKER AND ACTIVIST

People get too hung-up—they confuse love and sex as being
synonymous. It's not! The sex I have with my lover is different
than the animalistic sex I have with a guy on a set. I remember
where my bed is at night, and I remember the difference
between lust and love. Love is a commitment much deeper and
stronger than the act of sex.

SHAWN JUSTIN
porn actor

I find it so interesting that porn work
can still make you a social outcast in certain circles.
And that as an actor, creating a visual representation of
satisfying sex between consenting adults is usually
considered career suicide. It's much more likely
that you will receive enormous financial reward and
international acclaim for your vivid portrayal of
a cannibal or serial killer than for your portrayal
of a hot, happy, horny faggot! I hope that the multifaceted
nature of my entertainment career breaks down
a few walls and inspires some clearer thinking.
That would be something to be proud of.

MICHAEL
SOLDIER
porn actor

I'm the stereotypical porn writer.
I sit at my desk with a hard-on jerking off
while I'm writing. If it isn't hard then nothing good
will come out of it.

SCOTT O'HARA, PORN ACTOR, AUTHOR AND ACTIVIST

I watch so much porn, when I eat a banana, I spit on it.

ALEC MAPA, COMEDIAN

How in God's name can a porn actor be a role model? That's what's so fucked-up about our culture—we're actually starting to turn people into role models based on their physical attributes. How stupid is that? For example, during an interview at [the Cannes Film Festival] Nicole Kidman picked up a cigarette and the press went crazy about her being a bad role model. She's a fucking actress, not a crusader for social reform like Florence Nightingale. You know, what I do is intended for adults. By the time any of my fans can legally [watch my videos], they should be mature enough to make decisions based on their own experiences. And not the calculated risks I decide to take for their viewing pleasure. I mean, if somebody barebacks because Matt Sizemore looks cool doing it, don't you think they're going to bareback no matter who's doing it?

MATT SIZEMORE
porn actor

No cultural phenomenon expresses our confusion about the reality of the body better than pornography. Pornography exposes hypocrisy and power struggles over what the body is, how it should be used, and who decides both.

CONNER HABIB, PORN ACTOR AND AUTHOR

Pornography is rather like trying to find out about a Beethoven symphony by having somebody tell you about it and perhaps hum a few bars.

ROBERTSON DAVIES, AUTHOR AND CRITIC

Society has come a long way in the last decade or so, and a hell of a long ways in the past thirty years. Back then hardly anyone would admit to being a gay porn actor. Studios were being raided and having cameras and film confiscated and all kinds of stuff. A lot of people in the gay community now know someone who has done a video or two. I hate to say it but it seems like it's almost becoming mainstream and I think that's hurting the industry. Porn stars are supposed to be on some pedestal where the average Joe can't reach them. Not the guy next door, anyway.

STEVE O'DONNELL, PORN ACTOR

If we define pornography as any message from any communication medium that is intended to arouse sexual excitement, then it is clear that most advertisements are covertly pornographic.

PHILIP SLATER, AUTHOR AND CRITIC

In the old days, when you couldn't show sex on film, directors like Hitchcock had metaphors for sex. When you can show more realistic sex, the sex itself can be a metaphor for other parts of the character's lives. The way people express themselves sexually can tell you a lot about who they are. Some people ask me, "Couldn't you have told the same story without the explicitness?". They don't ask whether I could've done *Hedwig and the Angry Inch* without the songs. Why not be allowed to use every paint in the paintbox?

(On including explicit sex scenes in his film *Shortbus*.)

JOHN CAMERON MITCHELL, FILMMAKER

The pornography of violence, of course, far exceeds, in volume and general acceptance, sexual pornography, in this Puritan land of ours. Exploiting the apocalypse, selling the Holocaust, is a pornography. For the ultimate selling job on ultimate violence one must read those works of fiction issued by our government as manuals of civil defense, in which you learn that there's nothing to be afraid of if you've stockpiled lots of dried fruit.

URSULA K. LE GUIN, AUTHOR

Whenever I watch fisting,
it looks like someone digging for change in the couch.

ALEC MAPA, COMEDIAN

Nine~tenths of the appeal of pornography is due to the indecent feelings concerning sex which moralists inculcate in the young; the other tenth is physiological, and will occur in one way or another whatever the state of the law may be.

BERTRAND RUSSELL

critic, philosopher

SEX AND PORNOGRAPHY

What is porn anyway? Is it doing a shameful, crass act on camera, because if so, I screwed myself on camera years ago.

CHRIS CROCKER
internet celebrity

Gay porn was never dominated by gay models, and
in the case of Bel Ami, not even half of the employees
are gay. Gay porn should be more accurately called
"all-male porn." I don't see this necessarily as a cultural
difference—most of the models working for Corbin Fisher or
Sean Cody are straight as well. I know some gay models
in the U.S. who claimed to be straight to get a job with
some of the American studios.

GEORGE DUROY, ADULT FILMMAKER

When you write about anything involving porn, people click
on it. One thing I always wanted to do with my column was to
level the playing field: I can gush over a hot guy the way the
old Walter Winchell types would drool over some young starlet.
Porn is a great leveler, because everyone on earth is into it,
whether they admit it or not.

MICHAEL MUSTO, NIGHTLIFE COLUMNIST AND HUMORIST

Some people—men and women—seek
out violent and degrading porn because
violence and degradation turns them on.
They don't get turned on to violence and
degradation by porn. (How much porn do you
view that doesn't cater to your established
preferences?) Hardcore kinky porn meets a demand,
it doesn't create it. And the question we need to ask
when we discuss it isn't, "Should this type of porn be
allowed to exist?", but rather, "Under what
conditions is this type of porn being created?"

DAN SAVAGE, SEX COLUMNIST AND ACTIVIST

Get it up, get it in, get it off, get it cashed.
(On the duties of a porn actor.)

MICHAEL
BRANDON
porn actor

Pornography is supposed to arouse sexual desires.
If pornography is a crime,
when will they arrest makers of perfume?

RICHARD FLEISCHER, DIRECTOR

To porn stars who look down on other porn stars
for escorting—are you fucking crazy? I'm just confused is all.
You can do a scene for $300 and let a company make money
off you, but can't do a one-on-one for $300 knowing that it
won't be posted online? Still confusing—you can be on a set
with four to five people watching with lights and camera. You
can do that but not a discrete one-on-one private?
Hooker thinking! I can make money without having my face
plastered on (the) Internet. Meaning, I can hook and still
have a future without a porn past.

DIESEL WASHINGTON, PORN ACTOR

I live for shooting scenes where I bottom for hours for a guy
with an enormous dick, because the next week I feel like I can
do anything.

CONNER HABIB, PORN ACTOR AND AUTHOR

Controversy is the way to attract new customers. Nobody would
write about you simply because you are a nice guy shooting
good stuff. Michael Lucas could tell you something about this.
It took me some time to digest this lesson. So I suspect obscenity
charges would be good for sales.

GEORGE DUROY, ADULT FILMMAKER

I have all the curiosity of the anthropologist and the frank hope of the voyeur. Pornography's texture is shamelessness; it maps the limits of my shame... The message of pornography, by its very existence, is that our sexual selves are real.

SALLIE
TISDALE
author

1st edition
© 2013 Bruno Gmünder Verlag GmbH
Kleiststraße 23-26, D-10787 Berlin
info@brunogmuender.com

© 2013 JC Adams
Cover: Steffen Kawelke
All Artwork © 2013 Steffen Kawelke
www.steffenkawelke.de

Printed in Germany

ISBN 978-3-86787-526-4

More about our books and authors:
www.brunogmuender.com